Chapters

Introduction

2014 was a remarkable year for the London bus enthusiast. The 75th anniversary of the introduction of the RT and the 60th anniversary of the introduction of the Routemaster, plus TfL's 'Year of the Bus', produced many celebratory events in London. Added to this, a series of strikes by London Underground staff resulted in the use of heritage buses on main London routes, providing interest and pleasure for bus enthusiasts but unfortunately not for commuters.

A further significant event was the restoration of the wonderful B-Type bus, first in its original 1914 condition and then as a First World War 'Battle Bus'. All of these along with the annual running days and rallies, made 2014 a truly vintage year.

As it is likely to be some considerable time before there is another such year I thought it should be recorded. This book is my record. When preparing it I was reminded of the quality of the events, the variety of buses, the enthusiasm of the bus owners and the spectators and I had to keep reminding myself that all this had happened in one year. Will we ever see its like again?

I am most grateful to all the photographers who have allowed me to use their work to illustrate the various events. And of course, any errors are mine, not theirs.

Ken Carr
Boreham
February 2015

Cover Picture: In September 2014, for the first time in about 20 years all four prototype Routemasters were brought together at North Weald station at the Epping & Ongar Railway.   *Ken Carr*

Frontispiece: On a beautiful summer's day, RF281 is posed for the camera at Dunstable Downs.   *Keith Valla*

Below: A number events were organised to celebrate RT75. In November a running day was held on route 11. RT3062 heads along Threadneedle Street on an evening trip from Liverpool Street. *Thomas Drake*

Back Cover: Part of the incredible cavalcade to Regent Street passes over Westminster Bridge on 22nd June. *Albert Dawson*

During 2014 there were two strikes by the staff of London Underground. Both lasted two days and both resulted in a large number of extra buses being used in London to augment the normal service.

Much to the delight of many, heritage vehicles were drafted in alongside modern buses for the extra services. In fact many enthusiasts were calling the strikes the "London Bus Rally".

The general idea was to run the extra journeys in the morning & evening peaks, with the buses laying over during the day.

For the first strike on 5th & 6th February, the operators that supplied the extra buses were allocated different routes to run. Ensign did routes 25 & 38, London Bus Co. did route 29 etc.

By the time of the second strike, on 28th & 29th April, the experience gained from the first saw more heritage buses being used and some routes using more than one owner's buses. For example London Bus Company's vehicles on route 29 were joined by those from Timebus & Southern Transit.

Listed below are the planned allocations for both strike days. You won't be surprised to know that these did change during both strikes as TfL juggled their resources to provide the best possible service.

A third three-day strike was planned to start on the evening of 5th May, but the RMT union called it off. From an enthusiast's viewpoint this was a disappointment as even more heritage buses were due to be used.

However, a third strike affecting only the Central Line did take place on 21st August. Ensign provided 5 Routemasters to run additional journeys on route 25 between Stratford and Holborn.

Previous Page: Ensign's RT3232, awaits another trip on route 15 into Central London at Blackwall Station during the second strike. *Keith Valla.*

Allocations for the Strike on 5th & 6th February 2014. (Heritage)

Route	Types & No. of Buses	Owners
25	DMS (1), M (1)*, RMA(1)*, RT (3)	Ensignbus
29	RML (6/7)~, RT (3)	London Bus Co.
38	RM (2), RMC (1), RML (4), RT (1)	Ensignbus
139	RML (1)	Private
158	RM (2)	Stagecoach

Total no. of buses Wednesday = 25, Thursday = 26
* - M planned for use Tuesday, RMA planned for Wednesday.
~ - 6 RMLs Wednesday, 7 on Thursday.

Allocations for the Strike on 28th & 29th April 2014. (Heritage)

Route	Types & No. of Buses	Owners
2	RMC (1), RML (1)	London Bus Museum
2	RML (3)	RedRoutemaster
8	RML (1)	Routemaster South
8	RML (1)	Xelabus
15	DMS (1), M (1) ,RM (1), RMC (1), RT (3)	Ensignbus
29	RML (8), RT (3)	London Bus Co.
29	RM (1)	Southern Transit
29	RM (2)	Timebus
38	RM (1), RMA (1), RML (4), RT(2)	Ensignbus
205	L (1)	Southern Transit
205	RT (1)	Imperial
205	T (1)	Cardinal Buses

Total no. of buses each day = 39

During the second strike the 15 received some extra heritage attention, thanks to Ensign. RTL453 does a lap of Aldgate on its way to Blackwall.

Interestingly, Arriva's Enviro400, T24, working on route 135, carries the registration plate once allocated to Routemaster RM1324. *Keith Valla*

MCW Metrobus M1 was also allocated to the 15. In Great Tower Street it heads for Trafalgar Square, whilst RT3232 edges slowly eastbound. At times the eastbound traffic was so slow it was easy to chase the buses on foot! *Keith Valla*

M1 overtakes LT42 beside St Paul's Cathedral on a short trip from Trafalgar Square to Tower Hill. *Keith Valla*

During the February strike, M1 was used on route 25, between Stratford and Holborn. In High Holborn, the MCW starts another trip out to Stratford. *Keith Valla*

DMS2646 pauses at Aldgate on its way into Central London. Only for the February strike were heritage buses used on route 25. They were provided by Ensignbus who also used some of their newer buses on the extra journeys. For the April strike just newer Ensign buses were used on this route. *Thomas Drake*

After only 19 years in service, RTL453 was put into store and was finally saved for preservation in February 1970, 44 years later it pulls into Stratford Broadway. Behind it you can glimpse one of Ensign's bendy-buses, number 402, which was also used on extra trips on the 25. *Thomas Drake*

Although the full blown 3rd Strike scheduled for early May never occurred, on 21st August, strike action on the Central line resulted in Ensign providing a number of buses for TfL extras. Of interest to us was the decision to use

Routemasters on route 25 extras. ER882 and RCL2226 make a fine sight at Stratford. *Keith Valla*

Another from the August strike day. RML2734 emerges from Cornhill and crosses Bank Junction. RMA50 and RMC1485 were also used during the day on the route 25 extras. *Keith Valla*

For the February strike, The London Bus Company provided RMs & RTs for route 29 and this, DLP17, a DAF/President. The final DLPs ran in service on TfL routes at the end of 2014. Does this mean they are the latest buses that can be considered as heritage? The extras on route 29 ran between the Nags Head in Holloway and Trafalgar Square. *Thomas Drake*

On the second day of the first strike, RT3871 takes a break between workings in Great Scotland Yard. The 29 extras used this stand alongside the Routemasters from route 15H. *David Maxey*

RM909, has just completed a trip from the Nags Head to Trafalgar Square and is about to navigate the large roundabout before following the RM seen on the other side of the road back to Holloway. Incidentally, later in the year RM909 was chosen to be used for the 'Afternoon Tea Bus Tour' and has been fitted out with tables with facing seats and for a mere £45 you can enjoy a one and a half hour tour of the sights whilst drinking tea and eating cakes. *John Lidstone*

For both strikes Ensign were asked to run the route 38 extras. Although they mainly used Routemasters, the odd RT did turn up. The extras ran between Angel, Islington and Victoria. RT4421 heads for Victoria at Cambridge Circus. *Albert Dawson*

During the day, between operations, the Routemasters parked in Vauxhall Bridge Road. RMC1485 waits for a late afternoon trip to Islington. *David Maxey*

With the traffic almost gridlocked, RMA50 edges out from St Giles High Street onto New Oxford Street on a trip to Islington. *Albert Dawson*

11

For the second strike the 205 received a good selection of older buses. The extras ran from Mile End to Baker Street. Southern Transit's RM2179 was originally planned to work route 29. However, on the day, it was allocated to the 205. The RM picks up at St Botolph Street before continuing to the East End. *Thomas Drake*

At the same spot RTL1256, which was provided by Imperial Buses based in Romford, also heads for Mile End. Former Stagecoach Trident 17386 follows behind. *Thomas Drake*

Cardinal Buses' Titan, T961 was also used on the 205. This one runs in a fictitious Green Line livery, a colour scheme which the Titans never carried. It also carries the number GLT961. The green machine negotiates Aldgate. *Keith Valla*

Southern Transit also provided, Leyland Olympian L1 for the 205. L1 entered service at Stockwell in March 1984. In January 1985, whilst based at Croydon, it was allocated to South London being operated by the Cowie Group and was allocated to private hire work. In December 2000 the bus was bought by Connex Bus and based at Beddington Farm. Two years later it was sold to Green Light Travel. By 2009 Southern Transit had acquired L1 and it is now part of their private hire fleet. *Thomas Drake*

For the February strike, Stagecoach used two Routemasters as extras on route 158. RM2050 is about to depart Stratford on a run to Leyton. *Thomas Drake*

RedRoutemaster and the London Bus Museum provided Routemasters for use on route 2 in April. The extras ran between Brixton & Victoria. RML2760 was one of the buses from the Museum's collection that was used. *Luke Vjaksa*

In addition to the hired-in buses for the extras, heritage routes 9 & 15 continued to operate during the strike. RM1913 pulls away from a rather busy stand in Great Scotland Yard. *Keith Valla*

The 2014 running day at East Grinstead took place on Sunday, 6th April. The event is one of a number, run through the year by Country Bus Rallies.

As with previous years, a large number of heritage vehicles attended and operated a wide selection of services. The 2015 event takes place on the 12th April.

Previous page: RT1702 poses next to a Morris Minor 1000 in East Grinstead High Street. The RT ran in service between 1950 and 1972, the Morris Minor was registered in 1968. *Keith Valla*

Above: 'Merlin' MB90 pulls out of the High Street. This bus was in service from 1968 to 1978. Since then it has had a few owners. The current one, Peter Comfort, takes this bus to most of the running days held in the Home Counties. *Keith Valla*

Below: One of the highlights was the first appearance of the Bromley Bus Preservation Group's, Atlantean, AN53. It ran in London service from 1972 to 1988. AEC Reliance, RP90 is parked behind. *Keith Valla*

Above: RM1397 arrives back in the High Street passing Titan GLT961 which is awaiting a trip to Westerham. *Keith Valla*

Below: XF3 heads back to East Grinstead at Felbridge, this was one of eight experimental rear-engined Fleetlines bought in 1965. Initially all were allocated to East Grinstead and they lasted in service until 1981. XF3 is joined in preservation by XF1. *Keith Valla*

Another one from the Bromley Bus Preservation Group's vast collection, DMS1455. The vehicle is the group's exhibition bus and at East Grinstead it was provided for use as rally control. Behind is RF429 a regular attendee at the event. *Keith Valla*

RML2456 at Godstone Green beside the delightful Hare & Hounds pub. Notice the vintage car beside the front door. This Routemaster is one of the younger examples, entering service in April 1966, it was preserved in 2004. *Keith Valla*

22

PICTURE

PUTNEY COMMON

EVERY

PARSONS G^{RN} SLOANE S^{Q.}
PICCADILLY CIRCUS
SHAFTESBURY AVENUE
HOLBORN   BANK
KINGSLAND R^{D.} DALSTON LANE

POST

WEDNESDAY

22

FXT 288

In April 1939, RT1's body and chassis were joined for the first time. It's first passenger carrying run took place on route 22 in September 1939. Over the weekend of 12th & 13th April, the 75th anniversary celebrations of the RT began. The weekend's celebrations were held at two locations with a running day thrown in for good measure.

The event kicked off at Arriva's Ash Grove garage on the morning of Saturday 12th, where a mini open day was held. Thirty-two RTs turned up, including one, BDJ67, which was an RT built for the St Helen's Corporation.

From mid-morning, fifteen of the RTs headed out to spend the rest of the day working on route 22 between Homerton and Piccadilly Circus.

The following day the London Bus Museum held their Spring gathering at Brooklands, and most of the buses that appeared at Ash Grove made their way to Surrey to take part. Forty-five RTs appeared at the event and a short display road run was organised during the afternoon.

Previous page: RT113 pauses in Threadneedle Street.
Paul Godding

RTs at Ash Grove 12th April

RT1*	RT1777	RT3028*	RT3871*	RTW185
RT113*	RT1784	RT3062*	RT4421*	RTW467*
RT935	RT1798	RT3183	RT4779	RLH48*
RT1396*	RT2177	RT3238	RTL139*	
RT1431	RT2293	RT3254	RTL453*	plus St Helen's
RT1700	RT2688	RT3491*	RTL1076*	BDJ67
RT1702*	RT2775	RT3775	RTW75*	

* Buses that worked route 22

RTs at Brooklands 13th April

RT1	RT1777	RT2775	RT4235	RLH32
RT593	RT1784	RT3028	RT4494	RLH48
RT604	RT1798	RT3148	RT4712	RLH53
RT935	RT2083	RT3183	RT4779	
RT1396	RT2177	RT3254	RTL139	plus St Helen's
RT1431	RT2213	RT3316	RTW75	BDJ67
RT1700	RT2293	RT3491	RTW185	
RT1702	RT2494	RT3775	RTW467	
RT1705	RT2657	RT4139	RTW497	

Left: RTW75 en-route to Ash Grove as viewed from RT1700. *Ken Carr*

Below: A section of the impressive line-up at Ash Grove on the Saturday morning. *Thomas Drake*

Above: At one end of the garage yard all the green RTs were lined-up together. From left to right, RT3238, RT3491, RT3254, RT4779, RT1700, RT3183, and RLH48. *Keith Valla*

Below: Three early arrivals, RT3028, RT1700 and RT4779 wait to be called to their display position, three pigeons carry on enjoying breakfast. *David Maxey*

Above: After the Ash Grove gathering it was time for some action and from mid-morning a selection of RTs started to appear on route 22. RT3062 heads along King Edward Street, heading for Homerton. *David Maxey*

Below: RT3491 passes the Royal Exchange and approaches Bank Junction on a run to Piccadilly Circus. *David Maxey*

Above: Whereas trips on the other RTs were free. If you wanted to travel on RT1 you had to buy a ticket. This was to help contribute to the bus's restoration costs. Heading for Shoreditch, the pioneer negotiates the one-way system at St Pauls. *John Lidstone*

Below: RTs pick up in Bishopsgate beside Liverpool Street Station. Keith Valla, who has contributed a number of photos for this book, is driving RT1700 to Piccadilly. Another London Bus Company vehicle, RTW75, heads to Shoreditch. *John Lidstone*

Opposite: A wonderful view, RT3028 waits at the lights at the bottom of Poultry at Bank Junction. The skyline is dominated by St Mary-le-Bow church of 'Bow Bells/Cockney' fame. *Paul Godding*

Above: RT1396 is chased along Threadneedle Street by RT1. *Paul Godding*

On the Sunday, the rolling RT Roadshow moved to Brooklands and became part of the London Bus Museum's Annual Spring Gathering. RT2177 arrives in the display area on the old racing circuit passing RLH48. Both had been at Ash Grove the previous day. *Keith Valla*

Above: RLH32, owned by Timebus, is painted in Samuel Ledgard livery. It was painted blue in 2007 to celebrate the 40th Anniversary of the Samuel Ledgard Society. Four RLHs (2, 4, 6 & 8) were bought in 1964 to work in Yorkshire for Samuel Ledgard. Alongside is one of the former Reading Corporation Regents. *Keith Valla*

Below: During the afternoon many of the RTs were taken for a spin around Brooklands. The buses begin to form up alongside the Mercedez-Benz test track. *Bob Stanger*

DU CANE RD LADBROKE GVE
WESTBOURNE PK RD BAYSWATER
PADDINGTON MARBLE ARCH
OXFORD CIR BRITISH MUSEUM

7

ACTON L.T. MUSEUM DEPOT

NO ENTRY
RESTRICTED
AREA

NXP 997

The London Transport Museum based in Covent Garden is an excellent museum. However, it is restricted in what it can show due to a) it's size and b) the vast number of items owned by the museum. Therefore, there is a second much bigger site at Acton depot which is used to store most of their items, 370,000 of them!

The depot covers 6,000 square metres and provides storage in safe and environmentally controlled conditions. It houses everything from tickets through to buses & underground trains.

Normally the depot holds a couple of open days each year and also runs monthly guided tours of the site. At the open days there are sales stands and bus rides available.

The first event in 2015 will take place on 25th & 26th April, tickets are £10 which allows entrance on both days and rides on the buses. The theme for this event is the hidden engineering contributions that are vital to keeping London moving.

Previous Page: The museum's RT4712 was painted gold in 2002 to commemorate the Queen's Golden Jubilee. Arriva operated it on behalf of the museum and it appeared on various London bus routes and on special 'Golden Jubilee Tours'. When originally painted it featured a white band, but during a repaint in 2003 it was changed to 'royal' purple. Today it retains the purple band and can normally be found at Acton. *Keith Valla*

A general view of the road transport collection housed inside the depot building. Many of these buses are operational and from time to time appear at events in and around the capital. *Keith Valla*

During the first half of 2014, RM2 (right) was nearing the end of its rebuild back to original condition. This included the refitting of its original style front end. Next to it is Q1 trolleybus number 1768 and Titan T567. *Keith Valla*

RF537 and DMS1. Delivered in 1952 the RF was originally a Country bus but after four years of its 'green' period it became red in 1956. It survived in service until 1977. Daimler Fleetline (originally dubbed 'The Londoner') DMS1 entered service in 1971, it was stored in 1982 and donated to the museum in 1984. *Keith Valla*

Three more beauties, from left to right, Guy Special GS64, STL469 and AEC Q-Type Q55. The STL was saved by the museum back in 1954 after it had spent just under twenty years in service. The Q had been saved the previous year, it had entered service in September 1935.   *Keith Valla*

One of the highlights of the open days is the mini excursions run from the depot around the surrounding area. These usually last about twenty-five minutes and the price is included with the admission to the open day. In March 2014, RTW75 and RM1 alternated on the trips.   *Keith Valla*

On Saturday 5th May, 2014 Transport for London organised a heritage running day over routes 9 & 15. The event featured a number of highlights with Routemasters and RTs out operating between Kensington High Street and Tower Hill and a couple of buses ran trips to Barking and the former destination of route 9, Becontree Heath.

Previous Page: RMC1461 heads west on Cannon Street. *David Maxey*

Above: RT3251 on the stand at Kensington awaiting its trip east. This bus was new in 1950 and was used on the 'Final run of the RT Bus' in April 1979. It is now owned by Ensignbus. *Billy Birkett*

Below: Tower Transit's SRM3 was joined by Timebus' silver RM SRM7. The pair head east at the end of Knightsbridge and wait at the lights to go around Hyde Park Corner. *Billy Birkett*

Buses used during the 9H & 15H heritage day

Regulars	Guests
RM1204	RM1871 (SRM7)
RM1218	RMC1461
RM1562	RML903
RM1627	RT3232
RM1640	RT3251
RM1650 (SRM3)	RTW467
RM1776	
RM1933	
RM1941	
RM1968	
RM2071	
RM2089	

RT3232 pulls out of Barking garage heading back to Kensington High Street. A long trip indeed, but not as long as it would be if it was going to the other end of the original route 9, Mortlake. *Daniel Neville*

Below: A long way from its Westbourne Park home, SRM3 after arrival at Becontree Heath, Dagenham. *Billy Birkett*

Back in Central London, RT3232, RM1562, RMC1461 and RM1218. At this time the two red RMs were both regulars on the route. The RT is one of Ensign's and the London Bus Museum provided the RMC. *John Lidstone*

Below: The final shot from this event. RT3232 works a westbound service past Cannon Street railway station as a Stagecoach Routemaster heads for Tower Hill on a regular route 15H working. *David Maxey*

Throughout 2014, there were a number of garage open days held as part of TfL's 'Year Of The Bus' celebrations. The plan was for all the major London operators to hold an open day. Although mainly showcasing the current fleets, heritage vehicles did appear at each of event.

The first event was held at Stagecoach's Catford garage on 10th May and after further shows at Alperton (Metroline), Stockwell (Go-Ahead), Fulwell (London United), Potters Bar (Metroline) and Walworth (Abellio) the last one took place at Arriva Southern's Dartford garage on 7th September.

Previous Page: NS1955 inside Alperton garage shortly before the open day started. Ken Carr

Catford

Before the Catford event, a special ran from Shoreditch to Farnborough Village over the original route 47, it then ran back to Catford in time for the start of the open day. At Farnborough Village, West Ham's RM2060 awaits the return trip to Catford. *David Maxey*

Above: At the garage, the first and last Routemasters were in attendance amongst plenty of other heritage vehicles. On the forecourt from left to right are RM1063, RML2760, RM1 and G351. *Daniel Neville*

Left: All the open days ran trips on heritage buses. RLH61 is pretty full and ready to roll, note that the bus still carries its Canadian numberplate.
Daniel Neville

Slightly newer heritage. Titan T1030 and Daimler Fleetline DMS1426. Both types were allocated to Catford.
Daniel Neville

Alperton

Top: Metroline's Alperton garage open day took place on Saturday 7th June. RT1777, RM1005 and RTW335 stand in the yard. *David Maxey*

Below: Just like at Catford, trips were run from Alperton. RML903 passes Metroline's CELF at Perivale on one such outing. *Lawrence Abel*

Above: RTW335 has an interesting history. After withdrawal in 1965 it was exported to Germany and was used by a company to demonstrate their vehicle lifts. It was repatriated in 2004 by Imperial Buses. However, it was in need of serious attention and little work was undertaken on it. Therefore, in November 2009, it was donated to Ensign and it was sent to BusWorks in Blackpool for rebuilding. The restoration took four years and it was completed just in time for the bus to appear at Ensign's 2013 running day, it's first passenger carrying run for forty-eight years! *Billy Birkett*

Right: RML2589 poses outside the garage entrance, to the left can is MB641. *Billy Birkett*

Stockwell

Go-Ahead opened the doors to Stockwell garage on 21st June. An interesting selection of heritage vehicles was assembled for the event including Merlin MBA582 from the London Transport Museum collection and STL2377 from the London Bus Museum. *Keith Valla*

A view from RTL1076 entering the garage from the Binfield Road entrance past RTL139 and RM9. *Billy Birkett*

After the event, the opportunity was taken to stage this interesting line-up. RTL1163, RTL1076, RTL139, RTL453, RT1702, STL2377 and RM1063. *Daniel Sullivan*

Above: Throughout the day there were several road trips that ran a circular tour via Vauxhall Bridge and Westminster Bridge. RTL139 heads out on one such run. *Keith Valla*

Below: Two more RTLs on the circular service, RTL1076 (right) loads, whilst RTL453 heads along Lansdowne Way having just dropped off its passengers. *Keith Valla*

Above: Three more arrivals, RML2366, RML2323 and RM1357 from the Red Routemaster/London Bus 4 Hire operation run through the park after working on route X60. *John Lidstone*

Below: Thousands turned out over the weekend for the show. This is the view from the Finsbury Park end of the park, looking towards Manor House. RMs 1, 2 and 3 are nearest the camera. *Nicholas Hair*

One of the many highlights of the event was the appearance of a couple of Routemaster exiles. RML2663 is based in Neuss, Germany and is used for corporate hire. In order to be street legal in Germany, the bus has to be no more than 4 metres in height, therefore its roof has been replaced with one that is slightly lower than normal. It can be extended (as shown in the photo) to increase the headroom for guests. The bus was exported in May 2005 and this was its first visit back to London since. Owner, Herman Herfurtner made sure it was appropriately dressed for its marathon trip. *Ken Carr*

Johnny Svensson's RML2698 travelled from Sweden. It was exported in March 2009 and is now in use as a party bus in Stockholm. *Ken Carr*

Not 'Red All Over'! From left to right, RML2606 which is used as a customer hospitality bus by lighting company Aurora. RML2464, used as a mobile business school by NatWest Bank and RML2528 which was purchased earlier in 2014 by London Ghost Bus Tours. *Daniel Neville*

The X60 free service from Manor House ran a circular trip via Seven Sisters Road, Amhurst Park, Tottenham High Road before heading back down Seven Sisters Road at Seven Sisters tube station. Phil Swallow's RM5 heads along the High Road on an outbound trip. *Keith Valla*

Arriva's RM6 is about to turn into Amhurst Road with another packed trip. Both these photos were taken on the Saturday. On the Sunday both RM5 & RM6 remained on the display line in the Park. *Keith Valla*

SRM7 & SRM3 pose for the cameras on the Park's orbital road. SRM7 was heading out to work X60, whilst SRM3 just happened to come out to do a lap of the Park. Check out our *Routemaster 60* DVD, to see some interesting pacing shots of these two buses running through the Park.
Billy Birkett

Routemasters at Routemaster 60

RM1	RM811	RMC1507	RML2271	RML2498
RM2	RM848	RM1620	RML2276	RML2514
RML3	RM857	SRM3	RML2284	RML2516
RM5	RML883	RM1699	RML2291	RML2528
RM6	RML898	RM1804	RML2304	RML2539
RM7	RML903	RM1822	RML2306	RML2544
RM8	RM938	RM1840	RML2310	RML2583
RM9	RM999	SRM7	RML2323	RML2589
RM16	RM1000	RM1955	RML2334	RML2606
RM44	RM1005	RM1990	RML2344	RML2620
RM66	RM1033	RM1993	RML2352	RML2660
RM108	RM1063	RM2037	RML2363	RML2663
RM116	RM1086	RM2060	RML2364	RML2683
RM188	RM1138	RM2097	RML2366	RML2698
RM238	RM1274	RM2116	RML2368	RML2699
RM254	RM1348	RM2173	RML2391	RML2715
RM275	RM1357	RM2179	RML2393	RML2731
RM291	RM1368	RM2180	RML2394	RML2740
RM308	RM1394	RM2208	RML2396	RML2741
RM349	RM1397	RM2213	RML2400	RML2751
RM357	RM1403	RM2217	RML2412	RML2755
RM471	RM1449	RCL2226	RML2440	RML2760
RM479	RMC1462	RCL2229	RML2452	BEA1
RM545	RMC1476	RCL2233	RML2464	RMA58
RM613	RMC1485	RML2262	RML2468	RMF2771
RM752	RMC1486	RML2266	RML2478	FRM1
RM765	RMC1497	RML2267	RML2494	

In January 2014, it was announced that Heritage route 9 would be withdrawn in July. The route was set up alongside the 15H as a tourist attraction following the withdrawal from normal service of the Routemasters in 2005.

Originally route 9H, operated by First, ran from Aldwych to the Royal Albert Hall. In 2010 when it came up for tender this was changed to run from Trafalgar Square to Kensington High Street. First were once again awarded the operating contract, which transferred to Tower Transit upon their purchase of First's Westbourne Park operations in 2013.

The reason given for the route's withdrawal was that the travelling numbers were declining, with those travelling for leisure purposes opting for the 'New Routemasters' operating on route 9. The cost of the subsidy to run the 9H operation was put at over £1million.

The final day was 25th July 2014.

Previous page: RM1627 about to depart Scotland Place on the final trip. *Billy Birkett*

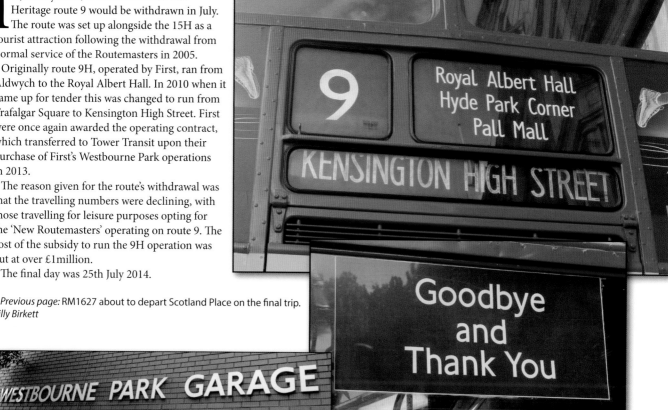

On the morning of the last day, before it started raining, hard, RM1562 awaits the lights at Trafalgar Square, before running to the stand at Great Scotland Yard. *Matthew Wharmby*

At the other end of the route, in Kensington, the two oldest Routemasters from Tower Transit's fleet, RM1218 and RM1204, await their final trips.

Interestingly, many of the trips during the final day weren't too busy which seemed to support TfL's decision to withdraw the service. *Matthew Wharmby*

By the early evening many more people were riding on the final services. RM1627 heads down St James's Street on its penultimate journey. Note the farewell blinds and ribbons on the mirrors. *David Maxey*

SRM3 worked the final eastbound journey. It pulls away from the last stop, on its last journey en route to Trafalgar Square in Pall Mall. After dropping off its last passengers it headed straight back, empty, to Westbourne Park.
David Maxey

This left RM1627 to work the very final journey. Just after 7pm, it pulled away from Trafalgar Square. It was joined on the last run by RedRoutemaster's RML2683 which ran in front empty. The pair head down Pall Mall.
David Maxey

At journey's end the pair were posed for photos in Kensington High Street. *Billy Birkett*

The scramble to get photos. A 'New Routemaster' from the 9 also stopped to join in. *Matthew Wharmby*

And below the line-up without the paparazzi. *Thomas Drake*

Above: The scene on the evening of 25th July at Westbourne Park. The RMs were lined up in the yard to await their fate. *Matthew Wharmby*

Below: Some of the final crew members get a memento of the day. *Matthew Wharmby*

The Battle Bus

A major highlight of 2014 was the restoration of the London Transport Museum's B-Type, B2737. This design was introduced to London's streets in 1910 and was the first successful mass produced motor bus, up until then most buses were horse-drawn.

B2737 was introduced into service in January 1914 on route 9 between Barnes & Liverpool Street. By the Autumn of its first year, it had been commandeered by the War Office and had been modified for use in France & Belgium as a troop carrier.

Upon return to London in 1918 it was used as a 'Traffic Emergency Bus', which saw it providing extra cover for congested bus routes. In 1922 it was sold for further use outside of London.

Previous page: The beautifully restored B2737 on display at Routemaster 60 in Finsbury Park. *John Lidstone*

Right: B-Types following modifications, await troops at Bolougne circa 1915. *London Transport Museum*

The bus's restoration began in early 2013 and was completed in June 2014. It has been restored using original parts from all over the world, bits that were missing or damaged were remade by craftsmen. B2737 was initially outshopped in it's original colours and it took pride of place inside Stockwell garage at their open day on 21st June. *David Maxey*

Not surprisingly, on the following day it was one of the stars of the cavalcade and Regent Street event. Afterwards it attracts plenty of attention as it heads past shoppers on Oxford Street. *John Lidstone*

Another shot from its first weekend out, B2737 heads along Lansdowne Road heading for Stockwell garage. The bus cost around £250,000 to restore and attended fourteen public events in its red livery. Then in September it disappeared from view whilst it underwent its transformation to a 'Battle Bus'. *Ken Carr*

SPEED 12

92 M.T.C. OY.
A.S.C

The transformation took place between the 8th & 11th September, by Transport Museum staff. Advertisements and signage were removed, the windows were boarded up, military headlamps fitted, the body work painted khaki and the interior equipped with a pickaxe and shovel.

The main picture shows it about half way through the process.

London Transport Museum

Above: The finished bus was unveiled to the public in Covent Garden outside the museum on 12th September. *London Transport Museum*

Below: It also was put on display outside the Hilton on Park Lane before the National Bus Awards in December. In between these two dates, the bus had revisited various locations on the Western Front. *Ken Carr*

SEPTEMBER 2014
FROM **LONDON**

TO **FOLKESTONE** 18TH
POPERINGE 19TH
YPRES 20TH
ZONNEBEKE 21ST
ARRAS 23RD
PERONNE 25TH
ALBERT 26TH

At Popperinghe, TfL's Surface Transport Managing Director, Leon Daniels poses in the bus between his official duties.

Right: Two days later, the bus in delightful surroundings at Passchendaele. *Lorraine Gray*

Below: Bus House Cemetery near Voormezeele. It got it's name from a bus that had broken down in no mans land. Leon & Sam Mullins, the London Transport Museum's Managing Director, laid a wreath here. The bus depicted on the front of the brochure below is possibly the bus that gave the cemetery its name. *Leon Daniels*

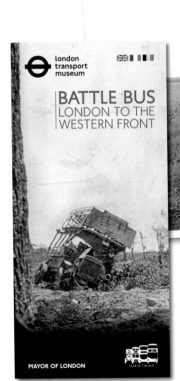

london
transport
museum

BATTLE BUS
LONDON TO THE
WESTERN FRONT

MAYOR OF LONDON

Below: A commemoration service was held at the Menin Gate in Ypres on the 20th September. *Lorraine Gray*

On the 18th & 19th October the Isle of Wight Bus Museum and the local branch of the Campaign For Real Ale, joined forces to expand the usual one day Autumn Running Day. The event centered around Newport with buses heading out in all directions, a wide choice of pubs were available on all routes.

A number of London heritage buses joined the fun and made the journey across to the island on the ferry.

Previous Page: Ferry across the Solent, RF281 is safely ensconced on the ferry, having been driven down from Essex. *Keith Valla*

Right: RT1702 also made the trip from the mainland. It has just arrived at Newport Bus Station with a trip from Bembridge on the east coast of the island. *Keith Valla*

Below: RF281 arrives back on the main land at Portsmouth and begins the long journey home. *Daniel Sullivan*

Above: RML2317 on show at Newport Quay alongside former London United's DT77 a Dennis Dart with a Duple body, which had a Plaxton front fitted after an accident.

Below: RF281, gleams in the evening sunshine at Carisbrooke Castle whilst working on route B from Hulverstone. *Keith Valla*

RM8 also made the trip across the water. It awaits its next trip at Newport Quay. *Keith Valla*

RF368 awaits another turn on route X at Newport Quay. Since withdrawal in 1977, this bus has had at least five owners. *Keith Valla*

RM1063 departs Newport Quay. The RM entered service in January 1962 and was withdrawn in March 1987. It was then sold to Wycombe Youth Council for a scheme that didn't materialise. It entered preservation in March 1990. *Keith Valla*

South Coast Rallies

Abbs Cross   Elm Park
Mungo Park Road
Sth. Hornchurch   Rainham
Wennington   Aveley

372

RT 3871

LLU 670

P393 OBA

Each year a number of running days take place at seaside towns located around the south east coast of England. 2014 was no different. We feature three that featured London heritage action.

Previous Page: RT3871 approaches Eastbourne pier on 3rd August. Four days earlier the pier had been badly damaged by fire. *Keith Valla*

Right: Twenty-three buses took part in the event. Four were London vehicles, the RT, RM1397 and a pair of RFs. The RM awaits departure from the seafront. *Keith Valla*

Below: RT3871 pauses for a photo in Sevenoaks on it's way back home to Ongar. *Keith Valla*

Above: A week before, there was the annual Worthing Sea Front Rally. A number of London vehicles turned up including these four Routemasters. From left to right, RML2393, RM188, RM254 and RM2097 create a temporary road block. *Billy Birkett*

Below: RT1777 and RM349 on show in the display area. *Billy Birkett*

Above: The Herne Bay event took place on 10th August, a week after the Eastbourne rally. RT3435 climbs away from the seafront with one of the trips around the town. *Keith Valla*

Below: RT4139 departs the main display area in the William Street car park and heads out on a trip around the town. *Keith Valla*

This section features a round up of some of the annual events such as the regular running days that took place in 2014. Plus some interesting one off events.

Previous Page: RT4779 pulls into Hemel Hempstead station during the running day on 17th August. *Keith Valla*

Right: RT604 arrives at Watford Junction station during the running day held in Watford on 30th March. *Keith Valla*

Below: Three more buses en route to the Watford event, RM6, STL2377 and RTL139 at Staples Corner. *Keith Valla*

Above: Routemaster contrast at the Harlow running day on 4th May. RMC1507 and RM1397 arrive at the bus station. *Keith Valla*

Below: RF673 and RF539 exchange passengers at Mulberry Green, before a run back to Harlow on 4th May. *Keith Valla*

Above: Leyland Titan T66 made an appearance at Potters Bar open day on 5th July. It has been restored into the General livery it carried between July 1983 and February 1984. *Mark McWalter*

Below: Another Leyland product, LS35 at the North Weald rally. This one has been restored in its 1989 livery which was applied for working the 'Docklands Express'. *Keith Valla*

Right: RM1000 rarely carries passengers. However, it did at the Alton Bus Rally on 20th July and proved very popular. The bus is still carrying it's Routemaster 60 blinds from the previous weekend.
Keith Valla

Below: RF26 returned to the rally scene in 2014. On 17th August it took part in the Hemel Hempstead running day. It has just arrived in the picturesque Sarratt village.
Thomas Drake

Above: A rather full Hemel Hempstead bus station on 17th August. RT4779 passes MB90 as it heads off on route 320. *Keith Valla*

Below: Another 2014 debutant was Atlantean, AN262. It worked at the Amersham running day on 5th October. *Thomas Drake*

Above: On 31st May the 85th anniversary of the Cheltenham District Traction Co. was celebrated. The event also doubled as a retirement bash for the company's Managing Director, Ian Manning who was an early committee member of the Routemaster Association. Therefore, a few RMs turned up. RML2657 arrives at Gloucester bus station. *Billy Birkett*

Left: RM835 spent four years working in Scotland following its withdrawal from London in 1986, hence it being preserved in Clydeside livery. *Billy Birkett*

Right: Stagecoach London's RM652 made the trip from West Ham to take part in the event. It was also joined on the trip by RML2760 which is on long term loan to the London Bus Museum. *Billy Birkett*

Above: On 26th October, two RTs (RT4779 & RT1700) appeared on TfL routes 406 and 418. A third bus RT3148 ran on photographers specials on route 406A express. *Thomas Drake*

Below: On 18th November, a private run took RM857 out on a few routes in South Essex. At Stapleford Abbots whilst pretending to be a 175A it meets up with a slightly older form of transport. *Keith Valla*

Right: Ailsa V3 made a few public appearances during the year, including the Canvey Island Bus Rally on 12th October.
The 1984 built Volvo has been restored two its original two-door, two-staircase condition.
Billy Birkett

One of the strangest sights of 2014. RML2335 was wrapped up in wool as part of a promotion for 7Up. 'Urban Knitter' (don't ask) Magda Sayeg was responsible for this, it took 3 days to complete and was carried out at Pinewood Studios. The bus spent a few days at the end of November driving round London, promoting the drink. During a rest break the Routemaster poses at Marble Arch. *Billy Birkett*

T499 became a TV star on 24 September when it appeared on the BBC's 'One Show' as part of a piece about bus passes. The feature also featured some filming from Showbus. The photo above shows the set-up, the photo below shows the bus just before it appeared on the small screen. *Thomas Drake*

Imberbus

In 2009, a group of bus industry professionals achieved a long standing ambition to run a vintage bus service from Warminster in Wiltshire, to the abandoned village of Imber on Salisbury Plain. It proved to be so popular that it has now become an annual event, with most journeys continuing across the Plain to parts of Wiltshire rarely seen by public transport users.

The 2014 Imberbus service on 25th August saw seven former London Transport Routemaster buses (together with three modern ones) providing a half hourly bus service from Warminster Station to Imber and other isolated locations on the Salisbury Plain. As the buses were providing an ordinary bus service, there was no need to book in advance – passengers just turned up and paid the conductor on the bus.

Previous Page: Sir Peter Hendy's RM1005 at Gore Cross. *Billy Birkett*

Above: Gore Cross located to the east of Imber is used as an interchange. RML2344, RML2665 and RCL2226, with open-top RM1510 at the back await their next trip over Salisbury Plain via Imber. *Thomas Drake*

Left: RML2665 and RM1978 head through Warminster. *Billy Birkett*

Below: At Sack Hill RM1978 and LT246 pose beside The Royal Tank Regiment's gate guardian. *Billy Birkett*

For 2014, Showbus returned to the Imperial War Museum at Duxford. In 2013 it had been held at Long Marston. The diamond Jubilee of the Routemaster was one of the themes for 2014 and a number of RMs attended the show. In addition there was plenty to interest the London heritage enthusiast, plus of course the Visions sales stands.

Previous Page: RT2293 arrives at Showbus. *David Maxey*

Right: As usual we had some buses as part of our Visions stand, this year there were eventually five! Stagecoach provided a Scania, Enviro400, an Enviro200 and a 'New Routemaster' and as we were selling the official Routemaster 60 merchandise we also acquired RML2674, which then got plastered in banners. *Ken Carr*

Below: RM7 made a reappearance on the rally scene in 2014, initially at RM60 and then at Showbus. It hadn't been out since RM50 in 2004! *David Maxey*

Top: A couple of RM celebs. RMF1254 the original forward door Routemaster delivered in 1962 and RM1000 pose outside the American War Museum at Duxford. *Keith Valla*

Below: RM2208 in it's representation of the 'Shillibeer' livery and RM1822 recently repainted into South London livery. *Keith Valla*

Titan, T40 is in need of some bodywork attention. The bus was new in July 1979, withdrawal came in March 2001 from Catford garage. *Billy Birkett*

RTW497 is also in need of some bodywork attention. This one was new in 1950 and lasted in service until 1966.
Billy Birkett

The newly refurbished Metro-Scania Metropolitan, MD60, now owned by Ensignbus, made its debut at Showbus 2014.
Thomas Drake

Above: The aforementioned rain hammers down at Aldwych, RTW75 heads for Chelsea. *Mark McWalter*

Below: RT1700 pulls away from the original route 11 terminus at Brook Green, Hammersmith and passes RTW75 which will run a shortened trip to Aldwych. *Keith Valla*

Top: If you wanted to travel on RT1 there was a charge of £5. It was shadowed by RTL139 during the day for those that didn't want to pay the surcharge. At the Pimlico Road and Buckingham Palace Road junction, it has been temporarily separated from its running partner and is being followed by RM898 on a short trip to Victoria. The RM was substituting for an unavailable RT. *Keith Valla.*

Bottom: More evidence of the bunching that occurred at times during the day. RT1 and RTL139 call at Aldwych with trips to Liverpool Street. RTW335 is right behind and will terminate here, before heading back to Chelsea. *Billy Birkett*

Above: RTL139 heads along The Strand. Note the conductor in period dress hanging off the back. Behind the RT, RM2050 nears the end of its journey on a heritage route 15 working. *Matthew Wharmby*

Below: RTW335 in Pimlico Road on a Hammersmith to Aldwych journey. *Keith Valla*

Above: RT3491 negotiates the surprisingly quiet roundabout at Trafalgar Square. *Matthew Wharmby*

Below: RT3232 on the stand at Chelsea Worlds End prior to heading back to Aldwych. *Matthew Wharmby*

Above: More of the 'green' participants. RT4779 heads along The Strand.
Matthew Wharmby

Below: RT3228 waits time at the Chelsea stand.   *Matthew Wharmby*

Above: The evening service between Victoria and Liverpool Street was operated by three buses. RT3062 heads down Ludgate Hill past St Paul's Cathedral.   *Billy Birkett.*

Below: RT3062 and RTL1076 pose alongside the Bank of England in Threadneedle Street.   *Keith Valla*

Poppy Day

E ach year, there are normally a couple of Routemasters used on former routes to raise money for the Royal British Legion's 'Poppy Appeal'. The 2014 event took place on 7th November and featured RML903 on route 4 and RM1005 on route 188.

Previous Page: RML903 prior to departing Finsbury Park for Waterloo on route 4. *Keith Valla*

Top: With the Cutty Sark in the background RM1005 rolls through Greenwich. *Keith Valla*

Bottom: RM1005 after arrival at Russell Square. *Keith Valla*

The final big event of the year was Ensign's running day, featuring many of their fine collection of heritage buses. The 2014 event took place on 6th December. Three routes were in operation, each with a half-hourly frequency. This resulted in an impressive one hundred and fifteen journeys operated during the day.

Previous page: RTL453 awaits departure from Upminster station on an X55 trip. The route runs to Gravesend via Lakeside, the Dartford crossing and Bluewater. *John Lidstone*

Right: RT1499 on route X81. This route ran between Grays and Shenfield via Lakeside, the Ockendons and Brentwood.
Mark McWalter

Below: RP90 works route X86 which linked Brentwood and Upminster and provided a useful link between the other two services. *Bob Stanger*

Below: RM1843 was rather popular, it was its first day back in service following restoration. The bus had been repatriated from the USA in 2012. It arrives at Lakeside. *Mark McWalter*

Above: RT1431 heels over as it enters Lakeside bus station. *John Lidstone*

Below: M1 heads through South Ockendon on a trip from Shenfield. *Thomas Drake*

Above: The beautiful RT8 on X55 departing Lakeside bus station. *Mark McWalter*

Left: RLH61 on X55 heads for Lakeside bus station on its journey from Upminster. *Mark McWalter*